for Lent 2020

P9-EDN-180

SACRED SPACE

from the website www.sacredspace.ie

Prayer from the Irish Jesuits

LOYOLA PRESS.
A JESUIT MINISTRY
Chicago

LOYOLA PRESS.
A JESUIT MINISTRY

3441 N. Ashland Avenue
Chicago, Illinois 60657
(800) 621-1008
www.loyolapress.com

Cover art credit: Tanor/iStock/Getty Images.

ISBN: 978-0-8294-4898-6

Printed in the United States of America.
19 20 21 22 23 24 Versa 10 9 8 7 6 5 4 3 2 1

Contents

The Presence of God

Bless all who worship you, almighty God,
from the rising of the sun to its setting:
from your goodness enrich us,
by your love inspire us,
by your Spirit guide us,
by your power protect us,
in your mercy receive us,
now and always.

How to Use This Booklet

During each week of Lent, begin by reading the "Something to think and pray about each day this week." Then proceed through "The Presence of God," "Freedom," and "Consciousness" steps to prepare yourself to hear the Word of God in your heart. In the next step, "The Word," turn to the Scripture reading for each day of the week. Inspiration points are provided if you need them. Then return to the "Conversation" and "Conclusion" steps. Follow this process every day of Lent.

February 26—February 29

Something to think and pray about each day this week:

Love continually flows back and forth between God and me because that is the nature of love—it is reciprocal. Such love begins with God, and in freedom I am invited to accept this love to make my corresponding loving response. Each day I desire to know with ever-increasing joy that I am loved unconditionally. My response to this deepening interior knowledge of the heart is to love God in return through my praise, reverence, and service.

—Casey Beaumier, SJ, *A Purposeful Path*

The Presence of God

"Be still, and know that I am God!" Lord, your words lead us to the calmness and greatness of your presence.

Freedom

"In these days, God taught me as a schoolteacher teaches a pupil" (Saint Ignatius). I remind myself that there are things God has to teach me yet, and I ask for the grace to hear them and let them change me.

Consciousness

How am I really feeling? Lighthearted? Heavyhearted?
I may be very much at peace, happy to be here.
Equally, I may be frustrated, worried, or angry.
I acknowledge how I really am. It is the real me whom the Lord loves.

The Word

God speaks to each of us individually. I listen attentively to hear what he is saying to me. Read the text a few times, then listen. (Please turn to the Scripture on the following pages. Inspiration points are there, should you need them. When you are ready, return here to continue.)

Conversation

Do I notice myself reacting as I pray with the word of God? Do I feel challenged, comforted, angry? Imagining Jesus sitting or standing by me, I speak out my feelings, as one trusted friend to another.

Conclusion

I thank God for these moments we have spent together and for any insights I have been given concerning the text.

Wednesday 26th February
Ash Wednesday
Matthew 6:1–6, 16–18

"Beware of practicing your piety before others in order to be seen by them; for then you have no reward from your Father in heaven. So whenever you give alms, do not sound a trumpet before you, as the hypocrites do in the synagogues and in the streets, so that they may be praised by others. Truly I tell you, they have received their reward. But when you give alms, do not let your left hand know what your right hand is doing, so that your alms may be done in secret; and your Father who sees in secret will reward you. And whenever you pray, do not be like the hypocrites; for they love to stand and pray in the synagogues and at the street corners, so that they may be seen by others. Truly I tell you, they have received their reward. But whenever you pray, go into your room and shut the door and pray to your Father who is in secret; and your Father who sees in secret will reward you. And whenever you fast, do not look dismal, like the hypocrites, for they disfigure their faces so as to show others that they are fasting. Truly I tell you, they have received their reward. But when you fast, put oil on your head and wash your face, so that your fasting may be seen not by others but by your Father who is in secret; and your Father who sees in secret will reward you."

- Today is Ash Wednesday, the beginning of Lent, when we prepare for the celebration of Holy Week and Easter. Let's increase our times of prayer during these six weeks of Lent.

- Why do you think Jesus encourages us to be private in our prayers? What do you see as the dangers of making our inner life more public?

Thursday 27th February
Luke 9:22–25

[Jesus said to his disciples:] "The Son of Man must undergo great suffering, and be rejected by the elders, chief priests, and scribes, and be killed, and on the third day be raised." Then he said to them all, "If any want to become my followers, let them deny themselves and take up their cross daily and follow me. For those who want to save their life will lose it, and those who lose their life for my sake will save it. What does it profit them if they gain the whole world, but lose or forfeit themselves?"

- Life holds so many challenges: the losses and daily disappointments that come my way. Do I despair, fall apart, and give up? Or do I rise to challenges and shoulder my crosses with courage, knowing that Jesus shares the load, thereby filling me with contentment, even joy?

- What do I think Jesus means by the statement "those who lose their life for my sake will save it"? I ponder this statement in my prayer today.

Friday 28th February
Matthew 9:14–15

Then the disciples of John came to Jesus, saying, "Why do we and the Pharisees fast often, but your disciples do not fast?" And Jesus said to them, "The wedding guests cannot mourn as long as the bridegroom is with them, can they? The days will come when the bridegroom is taken away from them, and then they will fast."

- Spend some time each day allowing the joy of God to fill your heart. Spend some time mourning with him, as joy is lost for so many. Any fasting is to remind us that the Lord of all joy suffers in his people, perhaps in people who are near to us. Prayer brings us near to others and near to God.

- Here Jesus uses the notion of fasting to reveal that the God whom the Jews hunger for has arrived. Rejoicing, not mourning, is the appropriate response to the presence of divine mercy revealed in Jesus. Lord, this Lent may my prayer and my fasting reveal my inner hunger for you.

Saturday 29th February
Luke 5:27–32

After this he went out and saw a tax collector named Levi, sitting at the tax booth; and he said to him, "Follow me." And he got up, left everything, and followed him. Then Levi gave a great banquet for him in his house; and there was a large crowd of tax collectors and others sitting at the table with them. The Pharisees and their scribes were complaining to his disciples, saying, "Why do you eat and drink with tax collectors and sinners?" Jesus answered, "Those who are well have no need of a physician, but those who are sick; I have come to call not the righteous but sinners to repentance."

- "Who? . . . me?" Levi, a despised tax collector for the hated Romans, must have been astonished that Jesus should want him as a disciple. Are you seated at your table just now? Hear Jesus knock, asking, "May I come in?"

- Or, sit at the table in Levi's house and join in the great banquet with Jesus and all the other guests. How much Jesus loves to socialize at meals, to meet people where they are most at home or in places of joyful nourishment!

March 1—March 7

Something to think and pray about each day this week:

A public faith life may bruise your head. It can embarrass you, challenge you, and create large amounts of anxiety and fear—on buses, in restaurants, along roads, or in Wiccan barns filled with wands. This is even more difficult if you are twenty-seven and some of your friends look at you the way you looked at the Wiccan warlock selling toads. Yet, along with its bumps and bruises, toads and dirty looks, the key ingredients to having a public faith life still include generous heapings of joy and grace, love, wonder, and strength—the strength to sometimes do things you never thought you could do.

—Matt Weber, *Fearing the Stigmata*

The Presence of God

I pause for a moment and think of the love and the grace that God showers on me. I am created in the image and likeness of God; I am God's dwelling place.

Freedom

Lord, you granted me the great gift of freedom. In these times, O Lord, grant that I may be free from any form of racism or intolerance. Remind me that we are all equal in your loving eyes.

Consciousness

Knowing that God loves me unconditionally, I can afford to be honest about how I am.
How has the day been, and how do I feel now? I share my feelings openly with the Lord.

The Word

I take my time to read the word of God slowly, a few times, allowing myself to dwell on anything that strikes me. (Please turn to the Scripture on the following pages. Inspiration points are there, should you need them. When you are ready, return here to continue.)

Conversation

Sometimes I wonder what I might say if I were to meet you in person, Lord.

I think I might say, "Thank you" because you are always there for me.

Conclusion

I thank God for these moments we have spent together and for any insights I have been given concerning the text.

Sunday 1st March
First Sunday of Lent
Matthew 4:1–11

Then Jesus was led up by the Spirit into the wilderness to be tempted by the devil. He fasted forty days and forty nights, and afterwards he was famished. The tempter came and said to him, "If you are the Son of God, command these stones to become loaves of bread." But he answered, "It is written, 'One does not live by bread alone, but by every word that comes from the mouth of God.'" Then the devil took him to the holy city and placed him on the pinnacle of the temple, saying to him, "If you are the Son of God, throw yourself down; for it is written, 'He will command his angels concerning you,' and 'On their hands they will bear you up, so that you will not dash your foot against a stone.'" Jesus said to him, "Again it is written, 'Do not put the Lord your God to the test.'" Again, the devil took him to a very high mountain and showed him all the kingdoms of the world and their splendor; and he said to him, "All these I will give you, if you will fall down and worship me." Jesus said to him, "Away with you, Satan! for it is written, 'Worship the Lord your God, and serve only him.'" Then the devil left him, and suddenly angels came and waited on him.

- At his baptism by John, Jesus had heard the voice of God the Father identifying him, a young village workman, as his beloved Son. During his temptation, he must have reflected on the challenges of this radically new mission. Am I tempted, like Jesus here, to put my needs first or to seek power that will make it possible for me to accomplish my goals?

- Do I want to attract notice, to be popular? A sense of power is intoxicating. Do I want to be influential, dominating others rather than serving them?

Monday 2nd March
Matthew 25:31–46

"When the Son of Man comes in his glory, and all the angels with him, then he will sit on the throne of his glory. All the nations will be gathered before him, and he will separate people one from another as a shepherd separates the sheep from the goats, and he will put the sheep at his right hand and the goats at the left. Then the king will say to those at his right hand, 'Come, you that are blessed by my Father, inherit the kingdom prepared for you from the foundation of the world; for I was hungry and you gave me food, I was thirsty and you gave me something to drink, I was a stranger and you welcomed me, I was naked and you gave me clothing, I was sick and you took care of me, I was in prison and you visited me.' Then the righteous will answer him, 'Lord, when was it that we saw you hungry and gave you food, or thirsty and gave you something to drink? And when was it that we saw you a stranger and welcomed you, or naked and gave you clothing? And when was it that we saw you sick or in prison and visited you?' And the king will answer them, 'Truly I tell you, just as you did it to one of the least of these who are members of my family, you did it to me.' Then he will say to those at his left hand, 'You that are accursed, depart from me into the eternal fire prepared for the devil and his angels; for I was hungry and you gave me no food, I was thirsty and you gave me nothing to drink, I was a stranger and you did not welcome me, naked and you did not give me clothing, sick and in prison and you did not visit me.' Then they also will answer, 'Lord, when was it that we saw you hungry or thirsty or a stranger or naked or sick or in prison, and did not take care of you?' Then he will answer them, 'Truly I tell you, just as you did not do it to one of the least of these, you did not do it to me.' And these will go away into eternal punishment, but the righteous into eternal life."

- The Father delights in people who show kindly, compassionate, practical love to those in need.

- Saint Matthew's hearers struggled with what would happen to non-Jews, because they themselves were the Chosen People. Jesus says that with his coming into the world, everyone is a "chosen" person. Everyone is to be treated with limitless respect. Jesus is already present, but in disguise, in every person. What do I see when I see the needy? Do I focus on the hidden glory of others? How would I fare if human history were to be terminated today?

Tuesday 3rd March
Matthew 6:7–15

Jesus said, "When you are praying, do not heap up empty phrases as the Gentiles do; for they think that they will be heard because of their many words. Do not be like them, for your Father knows what you need before you ask him. Pray then in this way: 'Our Father in heaven, hallowed be your name. Your kingdom come. Your will be done, on earth as it is in heaven. Give us this day our daily bread. And forgive us our debts, as we also have forgiven our debtors. And do not bring us to the time of trial, but rescue us from the evil one.' For if you forgive others their trespasses, your heavenly Father will also forgive you; but if you do not forgive others, neither will your Father forgive your trespasses."

- Jesus addressed the Father in his native Aramaic language as "Abba," a child's term of endearment, like Papa, Mama, Dada. The Lord's Prayer flows from the Jewish synagogue prayers that Jesus would have recited. It's not just a prayer for Jews or Christians but is appropriate for all believers in God.

- True prayer is simple and trusting, sometimes without words: "Be still and know that I am God" (Psalm 46:10). It can be good to dwell on a phrase or to savor a single word.

Wednesday 4th March
Luke 11:29–32

When the crowds were increasing, he began to say, "This generation is an evil generation; it asks for a sign, but no sign will be given to it except the sign of Jonah. For just as Jonah became a sign to the people of Nineveh, so the Son of Man will be to this generation. The queen of the South will rise at the judgment with the people of this generation and condemn them, because she came from the ends of the earth to listen to the wisdom of Solomon, and see, something greater than Solomon is here! The people of Nineveh will rise up at the judgment with this generation and condemn it, because they repented at the proclamation of Jonah, and see, something greater than Jonah is here!"

- People are coming to Jesus looking for signs. He compares himself to Solomon and Jonah, who were signs from God in their lifetimes. He, however, speaks with greater authority than these. What signs in your life are leading you to Jesus? Who are your advisors, and whose voice do you listen to when you think about the deep meaning of your life?

- Jesus tells it as it is. When "the crowds were increasing," he challenged them to ask themselves why they were coming to see and listen to him. Why do I come to prayer each day? Something greater is here.

Thursday 5th March
Matthew 7:7–12

"Ask, and it will be given to you; search, and you will find; knock, and the door will be opened for you. For everyone who asks receives, and everyone who searches finds, and for everyone who knocks, the door will be opened. Is there anyone among you who, if your child asks for bread, will give a stone? Or if the child asks for a fish, will give a snake? If you then, who are evil, know how to give good gifts to your children, how much more will your Father in heaven give good things to those who ask him! In everything do to others as you would have them do to you; for this is the law and the prophets."

- In these short instructions for prayer, Jesus invites us to come before God with expectant hearts, asking for what we need. God is always listening to our prayers. "All things can be done for the one who believes" (Mark 9:23).

- Parent/child is only a metaphor for what happens in prayer. I know, Lord, that you always hear my cry, but I do not always understand your answer. I will still go on praying to you, happy to fall back on the "Our Father."

Friday 6th March
Matthew 5:20–26

"For I tell you, unless your righteousness exceeds that of the scribes and Pharisees, you will never enter the kingdom of heaven. You have heard that it was said to those of ancient times, 'You shall not murder'; and 'whoever murders shall be liable to judgment.' But I say to you that if you are angry with a brother or sister, you will be liable to judgment; and if you insult a brother or sister, you will be liable to the council; and if you say, 'You fool,' you will be liable to the hell of fire. So when you are offering your gift at the altar, if you remember that your brother or sister has something against you, leave your gift there before the altar and go; first be reconciled to your brother or sister, and then come and offer your gift. Come to terms quickly with your accuser while you are on the way to court with him, or your accuser may hand you over to the judge, and the judge to the guard, and you will be thrown into prison. Truly I tell you, you will never get out until you have paid the last penny."

- Jesus' message goes deeper than adherence to the letter of the law, which the Pharisees were preoccupied with. It is about embracing the gospel values of forgiveness and reconciliation.

- The standards operating in the kingdom of heaven are high! Jesus does not dismiss Old Testament teaching but goes to the root of things. We can be smug and content with our conventional good behavior. However, Jesus says to us, "But what about your anger? What about insulting someone? Do you despise anyone, ever?"

Saturday 7th March
Matthew 5:43–48

"You have heard that it was said, 'You shall love your neighbor and hate your enemy.' But I say to you, Love your enemies and pray for those who persecute you, so that you may be children of your Father in heaven; for he makes his sun rise on the evil and on the good, and sends rain on the righteous and on the unrighteous. For if you love those who love you, what reward do you have? Do not even the tax collectors do the same? And if you greet only your brothers and sisters, what more are you doing than others? Do not even the Gentiles do the same? Be perfect, therefore, as your heavenly Father is perfect."

- Jesus teaches his followers about a new criterion of love that is to be the standard for the early Christian community and for us. It is not enough to love those who love you. To truly live as a disciple of Jesus demands that we reach out with an all-embracing love to others, including those who make life difficult for us.

- "If we love one another, God lives in us, and his love is perfected in us" (1 John 4:12). Contemplate the wonder of God's unconditional love for you and ask for the grace to radiate that love in the different situations and activities of your day.

March 8—March 14

Something to think and pray about each day this week:

Be who only you are. Rise to what you dream. Do not cease to dream. Do not despair even though pain comes hand in hand with joy. That is the nature of the gift we were given. It is the most amazing and extraordinary and confusing and complicated gift that ever was. Never take it for granted, not for an instant, not for the seventh of a second. The price for it is your attentiveness and generosity and kindness and mercy. Also humor. Humor will destroy the brooding castles of the murderers and chase their armies wailing into the darkness. What you do now, today, in these next few minutes, matters more than I can tell you. It advances the universe two inches. If we are our best selves, there will come a world where children do not weep and war is a memory and violence is a joke no one tells, having forgotten the words. You and I know this is possible. It is what He said could happen if we loved well. He did not mean loving only the people you know. He meant every idiot and liar and thief and blowhard and even your cousin. I do not know how that could be so, but I know it is so. So do you. Let us begin again, you and me, this afternoon. Ready?

—Brian Doyle, *The Thorny Grace of It*

The Presence of God

Dear Jesus, today I call on you, but not to ask for anything. I'd like only to dwell in your presence. May my heart respond to your love.

Freedom

God my creator, you gave me life and the gift of freedom. Through your love I exist in this world. May I never take the gift of life for granted. May I always respect others' right to life.

Consciousness

I ask how I am today. Am I particularly tired, stressed, or anxious? If any of these characteristics apply, can I try to let go of the concerns that disturb me?

The Word

The word of God comes down to us through the Scriptures. May the Holy Spirit enlighten my mind and my heart to respond to the Gospel teachings. (Please turn to the Scripture on the following pages. Inspiration points are there, should you need them. When you are ready, return here to continue.)

Conversation

I begin to talk with Jesus about the Scripture I have just read. What part of it strikes a chord in me? Perhaps the words of a friend—or some story I have heard recently—will rise to the surface in my consciousness. If so, does the story throw light on what the Scripture passage may be saying to me?

Conclusion
Glory be to the Father, and to the Son, and to the Holy Spirit,
As it was in the beginning, is now and ever shall be,
World without end. Amen.

Sunday 8th March
Second Sunday of Lent

Matthew 17:1–9

Six days later, Jesus took with him Peter and James and his brother John and led them up a high mountain, by themselves. And he was transfigured before them, and his face shone like the sun, and his clothes became dazzling white. Suddenly there appeared to them Moses and Elijah, talking with him. Then Peter said to Jesus, "Lord, it is good for us to be here; if you wish, I will make three dwellings here, one for you, one for Moses, and one for Elijah." While he was still speaking, suddenly a bright cloud overshadowed them, and from the cloud a voice said, "This is my Son, the Beloved; with him I am well pleased; listen to him!" When the disciples heard this, they fell to the ground and were overcome by fear. But Jesus came and touched them, saying, "Get up and do not be afraid." And when they looked up, they saw no one except Jesus himself alone. As they were coming down the mountain, Jesus ordered them, "Tell no one about the vision until after the Son of Man has been raised from the dead."

- The disciples see Jesus revealed in all his divine glory. It is a special moment for them, as Peter confirms: "it is good for us to be here." The voice of God the Father resounding from the cloud has an important message to convey to the disciples, and us: "Listen to him." A listening heart is a heart warmed by the love of God and taught by his words. The one we listen to is the Son of God: Jesus, transfigured in his humanity.

- Prayer is better described as listening than speaking. Spend some time in prayer just listening to the mood of love and peace in God's presence.

Monday 9th March
Luke 6:36–38

[Jesus said to the disciples,] "Be merciful, just as your Father is merciful. Do not judge, and you will not be judged; do not condemn, and you will not be condemned. Forgive, and you will be forgiven; give, and it will be given to you. A good measure, pressed down, shaken together, running over, will be put into your lap; for the measure you give will be the measure you get back."

- What a beautiful, challenging Lenten program! Let us strive each day for the remainder of Lent not to judge or condemn; to forgive and tell others that they are forgiven; and to do one daily act of generosity. What transformed people we will be by Easter!

- Jesus stresses once again the primary importance of good relationships with others. The world would be a different place if we were merciful and noncondemning. Lord, my poor heart is very small, and it can also be very hard. Your heart is large and also very tender and compassionate. When I try to forgive others, my heart becomes a bit more like yours, and you swamp me with your overflowing generosity.

Tuesday 10th March
Matthew 23:1–12

Then Jesus said to the crowds and to his disciples, "The scribes and the Pharisees sit on Moses' seat; therefore, do whatever they teach you and follow it; but do not do as they do, for they do not practice what they teach. They tie up heavy burdens, hard to bear, and lay them on the shoulders of others; but they themselves are unwilling to lift a finger to move them. They do all their deeds to be seen by others; for they make their phylacteries broad and their fringes long. They love to have the place of honor at banquets and the best seats in the synagogues, and to be greeted with respect in the marketplaces, and to have people call them rabbi. But you are not to be called rabbi, for you have one teacher, and you are all students. And call no one your father on earth, for you have one Father—the one in heaven. Nor are you to be called instructors, for you have one instructor, the

Messiah. The greatest among you will be your servant. All who exalt themselves will be humbled, and all who humble themselves will be exalted."

- The Pharisees had great clarity about their beliefs: they allowed their belief in God to speak to them about their own worthiness and to judge the unworthiness of others. Our religious acts and attitudes are our attempts to recognize God's presence and power. In hearing God's response, we are rescued from proclaiming ourselves.

- I pray not for certainty, but for humility. I ask God to let me know that, in being least, I can allow God to raise me up. This is the only promotion that matters!

Wednesday 11th March
Matthew 20:17–28

While Jesus was going up to Jerusalem, he took the twelve disciples aside by themselves, and said to them on the way, "See, we are going up to Jerusalem, and the Son of Man will be handed over to the chief priests and scribes, and they will condemn him to death; then they will hand him over to the Gentiles to be mocked and flogged and crucified; and on the third day he will be raised." Then the mother of the sons of Zebedee came to him with her sons, and kneeling before him, she asked a favor of him. And he said to her, "What do you want?" She said to him, "Declare that these two sons of mine will sit, one at your right hand and one at your left, in your kingdom." But Jesus answered, "You do not know what you are asking. Are you able to drink the cup that I am about to drink?" They said to him, "We are able." He said to them, "You will indeed drink my cup, but to sit at my right hand and at my left, this is not mine to grant, but it is for those for whom it has been prepared by my Father." When the ten heard it, they were angry with the two brothers. But Jesus called them to him and said, "You know that the rulers of the Gentiles lord it over them, and their great ones are tyrants over them. It will not be so among you; but whoever wishes to be great among you must be your servant, and whoever wishes to be first among you must be your slave; just as the Son of Man came not to be served but to serve, and to give his life a ransom for many."

- Jesus describes vividly the degrading ways in which he will be treated in his Passion. He does this to strengthen his disciples. When we decide to act lovingly in all we do, we become vulnerable. People will take advantage of us. But love will have the final word. We will be raised up as Jesus was. I thank God for this.

- Jesus, you abhor all forms of domination. The kingdom of God is to be a domination-free community. I can see how Christian churches fall into the trap of domination. But do I dominate anyone? Even in an argument? Do I even think I am better than anyone else?

Thursday 12th March
Luke 16:19–31

Jesus said to the Pharisees, "There was a rich man who was dressed in purple and fine linen and who feasted sumptuously every day. And at his gate lay a poor man named Lazarus, covered with sores, who longed to satisfy his hunger with what fell from the rich man's table; even the dogs would come and lick his sores. The poor man died and was carried away by the angels to be with Abraham. The rich man also died and was buried. In Hades, where he was being tormented, he looked up and saw Abraham far away with Lazarus by his side. He called out, 'Father Abraham, have mercy on me, and send Lazarus to dip the tip of his finger in water and cool my tongue; for I am in agony in these flames.' But Abraham said, 'Child, remember that during your lifetime you received your good things, and Lazarus in like manner evil things; but now he is comforted here, and you are in agony. Besides all this, between you and us a great chasm has been fixed, so that those who might want to pass from here to you cannot do so, and no one can cross from there to us.' He said, 'Then, father, I beg you to send him to my father's house—for I have five brothers—that he may warn them, so that they will not also come into this place of torment.' Abraham replied, 'They have Moses and the prophets; they should listen to them.' He said, 'No, father Abraham; but if someone goes to them from the dead, they will repent.' He said to him, 'If they do not listen to Moses and the prophets, neither will they be convinced even if someone rises from the dead.'"

- The poor are brought straight into the kingdom of God, while the rich have to endure the pain of conversion. I ponder the mysterious workings of God's providence. I pray for the rich that they be converted, and I ask to be shown how to share my own possessions with the needy.

- During Lent I try to hear the call to come back home to God. I join the great pilgrimage of people who, through the ages, have been called by Moses and the prophets to listen to the word of the Lord.

Friday 13th March
Matthew 21:33–43, 45–46

"Listen to another parable. There was a landowner who planted a vineyard, put a fence around it, dug a wine press in it, and built a watchtower. Then he leased it to tenants and went to another country. When the harvest time had come, he sent his slaves to the tenants to collect his produce. But the tenants seized his slaves and beat one, killed another, and stoned another. Again he sent other slaves, more than the first; and they treated them in the same way. Finally he sent his son to them, saying, 'They will respect my son.' But when the tenants saw the son, they said to themselves, 'This is the heir; come, let us kill him and get his inheritance.' So they seized him, threw him out of the vineyard, and killed him. Now when the owner of the vineyard comes, what will he do to those tenants?" They said to him, "He will put those wretches to a miserable death, and lease the vineyard to other tenants who will give him the produce at the harvest time." Jesus said to them, "Have you never read in the scriptures: 'The stone that the builders rejected / has become the cornerstone; this was the Lord's doing, / and it is amazing in our eyes'? Therefore I tell you, the kingdom of God will be taken away from you and given to a people that produces the fruits of the kingdom." When the chief priests and the Pharisees heard his parables, they realized that he was speaking about them. They wanted to arrest him, but they feared the crowds, because they regarded him as a prophet.

• We are the tenants in the parable. God provides everything we need to make our vineyard prosper. God gives us the freedom to run the vineyard as we choose—but it is God's. This is what prayer is about—coming to know the mind of God about our lives. What fruits will I produce for the Lord?

- One of the saddest statements in the Gospels is this innocent comment by the father: "They will respect my son." I am frightened to think what would happen if Jesus came into our world today. His message about the kingdom of God would put him in direct opposition to so many other kingdoms. He would become an enemy to be got rid of. Jesus, you were thrown out and killed. But you took no revenge. Instead, by your love you reconciled everyone with God. May I always wish others well and pray for them, even if they hurt me.

Saturday 14th March
Luke 15:1–3, 11–32

Now all the tax collectors and sinners were coming near to listen to him. And the Pharisees and the scribes were grumbling and saying, "This fellow welcomes sinners and eats with them." So he told them this parable: "There was a man who had two sons. The younger of them said to his father, 'Father, give me the share of the property that will belong to me.' So he divided his property between them. A few days later the younger son gathered all he had and traveled to a distant country, and there he squandered his property in dissolute living. When he had spent everything, a severe famine took place throughout that country, and he began to be in need. So he went and hired himself out to one of the citizens of that country, who sent him to his fields to feed the pigs. He would gladly have filled himself with the pods that the pigs were eating; and no one gave him anything. But when he came to himself he said, 'How many of my father's hired hands have bread enough and to spare, but here I am dying of hunger! I will get up and go to my father, and I will say to him, "Father, I have sinned against heaven and before you; I am no longer worthy to be called your son; treat me like one of your hired hands."' So he set off and went to his father. But while he was still far off, his father saw him and was filled with compassion; he ran and put his arms around him and kissed him. Then the son said to him, 'Father, I have sinned against heaven and before you; I am no longer worthy to be called your son.' But the father said to his slaves, 'Quickly, bring out a robe—the best one—and put it on him; put a ring on his finger and sandals on his feet. And get the fatted calf and kill it, and let us eat and celebrate; for this son of mine was dead and is alive again; he was lost and is found!' And they began to celebrate. Now his elder son was in the field; and when he came and approached the house, he heard music and dancing. He called one of the slaves and asked what was going on. He replied, 'Your brother has come, and your father has killed the fatted calf, because he has got him back safe and sound.' Then he became angry and refused to go in. His father came out and began to plead with him. But he answered his father, 'Listen! For all these years I have been working like a slave for you, and I have never disobeyed your command; yet you have never given me even a young goat so that I might celebrate with my friends. But when this son of yours came back, who has devoured your property with prostitutes, you killed the fatted calf for him!' Then the father said to him, 'Son, you are always with me, and all that is mine is yours. But we had to celebrate and rejoice, because this brother of yours was dead and has come to life; he was lost and has been found.'"

- Jesus told a rather elaborate story. If you could not use a story but had to create a rational argument, how would you explain what Jesus was trying to say?

- Jesus, remind me that I am part of the eternal sacred story. And teach me how to communicate to others that their individual stories are also sacred.

Third Week of Lent
March 15—March 21

Something to think and pray about each day this week:

Jesus clearly called us to compassionate service, especially for the people most in need. Melding our "being" with our "doing" proves a constant challenge. Ignatius reached a balance of prayer and action, realizing that one without the other puts our spirituality out of harmony.

Pedro Arrupe, former superior general of the Jesuits, remarked:

> Service is the key idea of the charism of Ignatius. It is an idea whose moving power achieved in the life and spirituality of Ignatius—even in his mystical phase—a total realization: unconditioned and limitless service, service that is large-hearted and humble. It could be said that even the Trinitarian "lights," which enriched his mystical life, rather than leading to a passive and contemplative quieting, spurred him to a greater service of this God he contemplated with such great love and reverence.
> (*Challenge*, 254)

—Jacqueline Bergan and Marie Schwan, CSJ,
Praying with Ignatius of Loyola

The Presence of God

I remind myself that, as I sit here now,
God is gazing on me with love and holding me in being.
I pause for a moment and think of this.

Freedom

"There are very few people who realize what God would make of them if they abandoned themselves into his hands, and let themselves be formed by his grace" (Saint Ignatius). I ask for the grace to trust myself totally to God's love.

Consciousness

Where do I sense hope, encouragement, and growth in my life? By looking back over the past few months, I may be able to see which activities and occasions have produced rich fruit. If I do notice such areas, I will determine to give those areas both time and space in the future.

The Word

Lord Jesus, you became human to communicate with me.
You walked and worked on this earth.
You endured the heat and struggled with the cold.
All your time on this earth was spent in caring for humanity.

You healed the sick, you raised the dead.
Most important of all, you saved me from death.
(Please turn to the Scripture on the following pages.
Inspiration points are there, should you need them.
When you are ready, return here to continue.)

Conversation
What is stirring in me as I pray? Am I consoled, troubled, left cold? I imagine Jesus standing or sitting at my side, and I share my feelings with him.

Conclusion
Glory be to the Father, and to the Son, and to the Holy Spirit,
As it was in the beginning, is now and ever shall be,
World without end. Amen.

Sunday 15th March
Third Sunday of Lent

John 4:5–15, 19b–26, 39a, 40–42

So he came to a Samaritan city called Sychar, near the plot of ground that Jacob had given to his son Joseph. Jacob's well was there, and Jesus, tired out by his journey, was sitting by the well. It was about noon. A Samaritan woman came to draw water, and Jesus said to her, "Give me a drink." (His disciples had gone to the city to buy food.) The Samaritan woman said to him, "How is it that you, a Jew, ask a drink of me, a woman of Samaria?" (Jews do not share things in common with Samaritans.) Jesus answered her, "If you knew the gift of God, and who it is that is saying to you, 'Give me a drink,' you would have asked him, and he would have given you living water." The woman said to him, "Sir, you have no bucket, and the well is deep. Where do you get that living water? Are you greater than our ancestor Jacob, who gave us the well, and with his sons and his flocks drank from it?" Jesus said to her, "Everyone who drinks of this water will be thirsty again, but those who drink of the water that I will give them will never be thirsty. The water that I will give will become in them a spring of water gushing up to eternal life." The woman said to him, "Sir, give me this water, so that I may never be thirsty or have to keep coming here to draw water." . . . The woman said to him, "Sir, I see that you are a prophet. Our ancestors worshiped on this mountain, but you say that the place where people must worship is in Jerusalem." Jesus said to her, "Woman, believe me, the hour is coming when you will worship the Father neither on this mountain nor in Jerusalem. You worship what you do not know; we worship what we know, for salvation is from the Jews. But the hour is coming, and is now here, when the true worshipers will worship the Father in spirit and truth, for the Father seeks such as these to worship him. God is spirit, and those who worship him must worship in spirit and truth." The woman said to him, "I know that Messiah is coming" (who is called Christ). "When he comes, he will proclaim all things to us." Jesus said to her, "I am he, the one who is speaking to you." . . . Many Samaritans from that city believed in him because of the woman's testimony. . . . So when the Samaritans came to him, they asked him to stay with them; and he stayed there two days. And many more believed because of his word. They said to the woman, "It is no longer because of what you said that we believe, for we have heard for ourselves, and we know that this is truly the Savior of the world."

- Jesus begins with his own physical thirst and ends up talking about the woman's soul thirst. What can I learn from this conversation about sharing the Good News?

- In speaking with a woman to whom he was not related, and to a Samaritan, who was considered apostate by the Jewish community, Jesus crossed two cultural boundaries. What boundaries do I face in a normal day?

Monday 16th March
Luke 4:24–30

And he said, "Truly I tell you, no prophet is accepted in the prophet's hometown. But the truth is, there were many widows in Israel in the time of Elijah, when the heaven was shut up three years and six months, and there was a severe famine over all the land; yet Elijah was sent to none of them except to a widow at Zarephath in Sidon. There were also many lepers in Israel in the time of the prophet Elisha, and none of them was cleansed except Naaman the Syrian." When they heard this, all in the synagogue were filled with rage. They got up, drove him out of the town, and led him to the brow of the hill on which their town was built, so that they might hurl him off the cliff. But he passed through the midst of them and went on his way.

- The people in question here were jealous for their community of faith. Jesus was including all nationalities in the care and the saving love of God. His audience was jealous of their own relationship with God and used it in many ordinary ways to keep others out of favor. They denied human rights to anyone outside their circle. Which people did my community teach me to exclude when I was growing up and learning who was "in" and who was "out"?

• Jesus is the one of universal welcome, his heart open in prayer and life to all, no matter their creed, nation, gender, age, or any of the categories with which we are divided from one another. I ask him to open my heart to be as welcoming as his.

Tuesday 17th March
Matthew 18:21–35

Then Peter came and said to him, "Lord, if another member of the church sins against me, how often should I forgive? As many as seven times?" Jesus said to him, "Not seven times, but, I tell you, seventy-seven times. For this reason the kingdom of heaven may be compared to a king who wished to settle accounts with his slaves. When he began the reckoning, one who owed him ten thousand talents was brought to him; and, as he could not pay, his lord ordered him to be sold, together with his wife and children and all his possessions, and payment to be made. So the slave fell on his knees before him, saying, 'Have patience with me, and I will pay you everything.' And out of pity for him, the lord of that slave released him and forgave him the debt. But that same slave, as he went out, came upon one of his fellow slaves who owed him a hundred denarii; and seizing him by the throat, he said, 'Pay what you owe.' Then his fellow slave fell down and pleaded with him, 'Have patience with me, and I will pay you.' But he refused; then he went and threw him into prison until he should pay the debt. When his fellow slaves saw what had happened, they were greatly distressed, and they went and reported to their lord all that had taken place. Then his lord summoned him and said to him, 'You wicked slave! I forgave you all that debt because you pleaded with me. Should you not have had mercy on your fellow slave, as I had mercy on you?' And in anger his lord handed him over to be tortured until he should pay his entire debt. So my heavenly Father will also do to every one of you, if you do not forgive your brother or sister from your heart."

- Forgiveness is never easy. Surely to forgive one's brother or sister up to seven times is pretty generous! After all, there has to be a limit, at least so Peter thought!

- Not so, according to Jesus: seventy-seven times. No limit, endless and ongoing. This is how the Lord loves you. "I forgave you all that debt"

(Matthew 18:32). Thank you, Lord, for forgiving me seventy-seven times and more. Give me the grace to forgive someone today.

Wednesday 18th March
Matthew 5:17–19

Jesus said to the crowds, "Do not think that I have come to abolish the law or the prophets; I have come not to abolish but to fulfill. For truly I tell you, until heaven and earth pass away, not one letter, not one stroke of a letter, will pass from the law until all is accomplished. Therefore, whoever breaks one of the least of these commandments, and teaches others to do the same, will be called least in the kingdom of heaven; but whoever does them and teaches them will be called great in the kingdom of heaven."

• It is not so easy to pray this gospel! "Do not think that I have come to abolish the law or the proph-ets." The heart of the Law was and is: "You must love the Lord your God with all your heart, and with all your soul, and with all your mind . . . [and] your neighbor as yourself" (Matthew 22:37, 39). Observing external laws is not enough. Jesus wants listening hearts, courageous, generous, and discerning. Hearts like his. Are you ever called to be prophetic by rising above peer pressure and speaking the truth in your heart?

- Lord, you were not turning your back on the past but deepening our sense of where we stand before God: not as scrupulous rule keepers but as loving children.

Thursday 19th March
Saint Joseph, Spouse of the Blessed Virgin Mary
Matthew 1:16, 18–21, 24a

[A]nd Jacob [was] the father of Joseph the husband of Mary, of whom Jesus was born, who is called the Messiah. . . . Now the birth of Jesus the Messiah took place in this way. When his mother Mary had been engaged to Joseph, but before they lived together, she was found to be with child from the Holy Spirit. Her husband Joseph, being a righteous man and unwilling to expose her to public disgrace, planned to dismiss her quietly. But just when he had resolved to do this, an angel of the Lord appeared to him in a dream and said, "Joseph, son of David, do not be afraid to take Mary as your wife, for the child conceived in her is from the Holy Spirit. She will bear a son, and you are to name him Jesus, for he will save his people from their sins." . . . When Joseph awoke from sleep, he did as the angel of the Lord commanded him.

- God called Joseph to let go of his own plans and put himself at the service of Jesus and Mary. We hear no words from Joseph in the Gospels, only mention of his being a just and generous man: his taking Mary into his home and his protection of Mary and Jesus. Joseph passed years in Nazareth, his faithfulness expressed in routine services that never drew attention to himself.

- Yet he had one important commission: "you are to name him Jesus, for he will save his people from their sins." Spend time resting in Joseph's company. He understands your daily tasks. Let him look lovingly at you and all you must do today. Be at ease in the presence of the one who lived in the presence of Jesus and Mary.

Friday 20th March
Mark 12:28–34

One of the scribes came near and heard them disputing with one another, and seeing that Jesus answered them well, he asked him, "Which commandment is the first of all?" Jesus answered, "The first is, 'Hear, O Israel: the Lord our God, the Lord is one; you shall love the Lord your God with all your heart, and with all your soul, and with all your mind, and with all your strength.' The second is this, 'You shall love your neighbor as yourself.' There is no other commandment greater than these." Then the scribe said to him, "You are right, Teacher; you have truly said that 'he is one, and besides him there is no other'; and 'to love him with all the heart, and with all the understanding, and with all the strength,' and 'to love one's neighbor as oneself,'—this is much more important than all whole burnt offerings and sacrifices." When Jesus saw that he answered wisely, he said to him, "You are not far from the kingdom of God." After that no one dared to ask him any question.

- The first commandment is to love God with all we have—not only with our hearts, but with our limbs. We need to embrace the Almighty in all we do. We are called to give him total love in a spirit of adoration.

- There are two commandments, even if they merge together. We have to love our neighbor (all people) as being part of ourselves. Especially their sufferings need to impinge on us. Our love should not be only for those who please us but also for those we don't like or who may be hostile to us. The most important thing in life is to have a loving heart, which is very demanding.

Saturday 21st March

Luke 18:9–14

He also told this parable to some who trusted in themselves that they were righteous and regarded others with contempt: "Two men went up to the temple to pray, one a Pharisee and the other a tax collector. The Pharisee, standing by himself, was praying thus, 'God, I thank you that I am not like other people: thieves, rogues, adulterers, or even like this tax collector. I fast twice a week; I give a tenth of all my income.' But the tax collector, standing far off, would not even look up to heaven, but was beating his breast and saying, 'God, be merciful to me, a sinner!' I tell you, this man went down to his home justified rather than the other; for all who exalt themselves will be humbled, but all who humble themselves will be exalted."

- The contrast between Pharisee and publican has entered so deeply into our culture that it is sometimes reversed, and people are more anxious to hide at the back of the church than to be in the front pews.

- How does the story strike me? I would hate to be the object of people's contempt. But Lord, if they knew me as you do, they might be right to feel contempt. And I have no right to look down on those whose sins are paraded in the media. Be merciful to me.

Fourth Week of Lent
March 22—March 28

Something to think and pray about each day this week:

You can't lead others if you can't lead yourself. But you can't lead others if you use power primarily to serve yourself and your ego. Leadership is not about you, it's about the rest of us—your family, community, colleagues, or customers.

"Get over yourself" is how we blunt New Yorkers put it. Pope Francis employs a richer concept: "Authentic power is service." The two phrases encapsulate a paradox of leadership. Leaders must dig deep within themselves, but that inward journey ultimately inspires them to leap beyond the shortsighted horizons that diminish so many leaders, who never see beyond my department, my company, my money, me, me, me.

Good leaders see farther. They feel called to transcend themselves and serve a greater mission than self-interest alone.

—Chris Lowney, *Pope Francis: Why He Leads the Way He Leads*

The Presence of God
I pause for a moment
and reflect on God's life-giving presence
in every part of my body,
in everything around me,
in the whole of my life.

Freedom
Many countries are at this moment suffering the agonies of war. I bow my head in thanksgiving for my freedom. I pray for all prisoners and captives.

Consciousness
Knowing that God loves me unconditionally, I look honestly over the past day, its events, and my feelings. Do I have something to be grateful for? Then I give thanks. Is there something I am sorry for? Then I ask forgiveness.

The Word
Now I turn to the Scripture set out for me this day. I read slowly over the words and see if any sentence or sentiment appeals to me. (Please turn to the Scripture on the following pages. Inspiration points are there, should you need them. When you are ready, return here to continue.)

Conversation

I know with certainty that there were times when you carried me, Lord. There were times when it was through your strength that I got through the dark times in my life.

Conclusion

Glory be to the Father, and to the Son, and to the Holy Spirit,
As it was in the beginning, is now and ever shall be,
World without end. Amen.

Sunday 22nd March
Fourth Sunday of Lent

John 9:1–41

As he walked along, he saw a man blind from birth. His disciples asked him, "Rabbi, who sinned, this man or his parents, that he was born blind?" Jesus answered, "Neither this man nor his parents sinned; he was born blind so that God's works might be revealed in him. We must work the works of him who sent me while it is day; night is coming when no one can work. As long as I am in the world, I am the light of the world." When he had said this, he spat on the ground and made mud with the saliva and spread the mud on the man's eyes, saying to him, "Go, wash in the pool of Siloam" (which means Sent). Then he went and washed and came back able to see. The neighbors and those who had seen him before as a beggar began to ask, "Is this not the man who used to sit and beg?" Some were saying, "It is he." Others were saying, "No, but it is someone like him." He kept saying, "I am the man." But they kept asking him, "Then how were your eyes opened?" He answered, "The man called Jesus made mud, spread it on my eyes, and said to me, 'Go to Siloam and wash.' Then I went and washed and received my sight." They said to him, "Where is he?" He said, "I do not know." They brought to the Pharisees the man who had formerly been blind. Now it was a sabbath day when Jesus made the mud and opened his eyes. Then the Pharisees also began to ask him how he had received his sight. He said to them, "He put mud on my eyes. Then I washed, and now I see." Some of the Pharisees said, "This man is not from God, for he does not observe the sabbath." But others said, "How can a man who is a sinner perform such signs?" And they were divided. So they said again to the blind man, "What do you say about him? It was your eyes he opened." He said, "He is a prophet." The Jews did not believe that he had been blind and had received his sight until they called the parents of the man who had received his sight and asked them, "Is this your son, who you say was born blind? How then does he now see?" His parents answered, "We know that this is our son, and that he was born blind; but we do not know how it is that now he sees, nor do we know who opened his eyes. Ask him; he is of age. He will speak for himself." His parents said this because they were afraid of the Jews; for the Jews had already agreed that anyone who confessed Jesus to be the Messiah would be put out of the synagogue. Therefore his parents said, "He is of age; ask him." So for the second time they called the man who had been blind, and they said to him, "Give glory to God! We know that this man is a sinner." He answered, "I do not know whether he is a sinner. One thing I do know, that though I was blind, now I see." They said to him, "What did he do to you? How did he open your eyes?" He answered them, "I have told you already, and you would not listen. Why do you want to hear it again? Do you also want to become his disciples?" Then they reviled him, saying, "You are his disciple, but we are disciples of Moses. We know that God has spoken to Moses, but as for this man, we do not know where he comes from." The man answered, "Here is an astonishing thing! You do not know where he comes from, and yet he opened my eyes. We know that God does not listen to sinners, but he does listen to one who worships him and obeys his will. Never since the world began has it been heard that anyone opened the eyes of a person born blind. If this man were not from God, he could do nothing." They answered him, "You were born entirely in sins, and are you trying to teach us?" And they drove him out. Jesus heard that they had driven him out, and when he found him, he said, "Do you believe in the Son of Man?" He answered, "And who is he, sir? Tell me, so that I may believe in him." Jesus said to him, "You have seen him, and the one speaking with you is he." He said, "Lord, I believe." And he worshiped him.

- The opening question of the disciples was, "Who is to blame?" This is a common question in the media today; perhaps it is part of my own vocabulary.

Jesus reminds us that sometimes no one is to blame but that difficult situations present an opportunity for us to be drawn into God's presence.

- Lord, there were times I was lost and found, was blind and then could see. Thank you. The man's blindness is cured, but the blindness of those who won't believe in Jesus remains. I think of how I grope, stumble, and am unsure of my direction unless I can rely on Jesus, the light of the world.

Monday 23rd March
John 4:43–54

When the two days were over, he went from that place to Galilee (for Jesus himself had testified that a prophet has no honor in the prophet's own country). When he came to Galilee, the Galileans welcomed him, since they had seen all that he had done in Jerusalem at the festival; for they too had gone to the festival. Then he came again to Cana in Galilee where he had changed the water into wine. Now there was a royal official whose son lay ill in Capernaum. When he heard that Jesus had come from Judea to Galilee, he went and begged him to come down and heal his son, for he was at the point of death. Then Jesus said to him, "Unless you see signs and wonders you will not believe." The official said to him, "Sir, come down before my little boy dies." Jesus said to him, "Go; your son will live." The man believed the word that Jesus spoke to him and started on his way. As he was going down, his slaves met him and told him that his child was alive. So he asked them the hour when he began to recover, and they said to him, "Yesterday at one in the afternoon the fever left him." The father realized that this was the hour when Jesus had said to him, "Your son will live." So he himself believed, along with his whole household. Now this was the second sign that Jesus did after coming from Judea to Galilee.

- This man believed Jesus' word *without* signs and wonders. His believing was followed by the wonder of his son's recovery, which led to his whole household believing.

- This is the first recorded healing miracle of Jesus. Do I believe in miracles? More important, do I believe that Jesus is "the greatest miracle of the universe? He is all the love of God contained in a human heart and a human face" (Pope Benedict XVI).

Tuesday 24th March

John 5:1–16

After this there was a festival of the Jews, and Jesus went up to Jerusalem. Now in Jerusalem by the Sheep Gate there is a pool, called in Hebrew Beth-zatha, which has five porticoes. In these lay many invalids—blind, lame, and paralyzed. One man was there who had been ill for thirty-eight years. When Jesus saw him lying there and knew that he had been there a long time, he said to him, "Do you want to be made well?" The sick man answered him, "Sir, I have no one to put me into the pool when the water is stirred up; and while I am making my way, someone else steps down ahead of me." Jesus said to him, "Stand up, take your mat and walk." At once the man was made well, and he took up his mat and began to walk. Now that day was a sabbath. So the Jews said to the man who had been cured, "It is the sabbath; it is not lawful for you to carry your mat." But he answered them, "The man who made me well said to me, 'Take up your mat and walk.'" They asked him, "Who is the man who said to you, 'Take it up and walk'?" Now the man who had been healed did not know who it was, for Jesus had disappeared in the crowd that was there. Later Jesus found him in the temple and said to him, "See, you have been made well! Do not sin any more, so that nothing worse happens to you." The man went away and told the Jews that it was Jesus who had made him well. Therefore the Jews started persecuting Jesus, because he was doing such things on the sabbath.

- The man on the mat is obviously ill, and yet Jesus asks if he wants to be made well. In truth, sometimes we prefer to remain as we are rather than change for the better. We fear what the change will bring, or we have grown comfortable with our "illness." I imagine Jesus asking me, right now, "Do you want to be made well?" What is my response?

- By healing people on the Sabbath, Jesus was breaking not the law of Moses but subsequent laws created to help people know how to fulfill the law of Moses. It can seem simpler to stick with rigid and complicated systems than to rely on our own discernment of what God asks of us. What discernment is required of me today?

Wednesday 25th March
The Annunciation of the Lord
Luke 1:26–38

In the sixth month the angel Gabriel was sent by God to a town in Galilee called Nazareth, to a virgin engaged to a man whose name was Joseph, of the house of David. The virgin's name was Mary. And he came to her and said, "Greetings, favored one! The Lord is with you." But she was much perplexed by his words and pondered what sort of greeting this might be. The angel said to her, "Do not be afraid, Mary, for you have found favor with God. And now, you will conceive in your womb and bear a son, and you will name him Jesus. He will be great, and will be called the Son of the Most High, and the Lord God will give to him the throne of his ancestor David. He will reign over the house of Jacob forever, and of his kingdom there will be no end." Mary said to the angel, "How can this be, since I am a virgin?" The angel said to her, "The Holy Spirit will come upon you, and the power of the Most High will overshadow you; therefore the child to be born will be holy; he will be called Son of God. And now, your relative Elizabeth in her old age has also conceived a son; and this is the sixth month for her who was said to be barren. For nothing will be impossible with God." Then Mary said, "Here am I, the servant of the Lord; let it be with me according to your word." Then the angel departed from her.

• Like Mary, I came into the world for a purpose. That purpose probably will not be revealed to me as dramatically as it was to her. Perhaps she heard God's message so clearly because she was comfortable with silence. Too often I fear the emptiness, the darkness, the silence within me. Yet it is there that the Spirit lives and works, even when my prayer seems most arid. God, help me go daily into the quiet of my heart, to meet you there, in love and adoration.

- Mary did not receive the angel's message as a total surprise; she was ready to engage in conversation with God's messenger. I turn to God in my prayer and try to see God's finger at work in my life. I draw inspiration from Mary's disposition.

Thursday 26th March
John 5:31–47

"If I testify about myself, my testimony is not true. There is another who testifies on my behalf, and I know that his testimony to me is true. You sent messengers to John, and he testified to the truth. Not that I accept such human testimony, but I say these things so that you may be saved. He was a burning and shining lamp, and you were willing to rejoice for a while in his light. But I have a testimony greater than John's. The works that the Father has given me to complete, the very works that I am doing, testify on my behalf that the Father has sent me. And the Father who sent me has himself testified on my behalf. You have never heard his voice or seen his form, and you do not have his word abiding in you, because you do not believe him whom he has sent. You search the scriptures because you think that in them you have eternal life; and it is they that testify on my behalf. Yet you refuse to come to me to have life. I do not accept glory from human beings. But I know that you do not have the love of God in you. I have come in my Father's name, and you do not accept me; if another comes in his own name, you will accept him. How can you believe when you accept glory from one another and do not seek the glory that comes from the one who alone is God? Do not think that I will accuse you before the Father; your accuser is Moses, on whom you have set your hope. If you believed Moses, you would believe me, for he wrote about me. But if you do not believe what he wrote, how will you believe what I say?"

- Jesus appeals to the minds of those who seek to disregard him. He reminds them of what they have seen, of the witnesses they have heard, and of the words of the prophets. I pray that I be blessed with deeper faith as I review the evidence to which Jesus draws my attention. As I believe in Jesus who was sent by God, the word of God is alive in me.

- John the Baptist prepared the way for people to hear Jesus. He brought people near to God, and some of them recognized Jesus when he arrived. Some people we meet make it easier to recognize Jesus. It is good to have met people who are like Jesus—just as John the Baptist prepared the way of Jesus by the way he lived. Give thanks for such people in prayer!

Friday 27th March

John 7:1–2, 10, 25–30

After this Jesus went about in Galilee. He did not wish to go about in Judea because the Jews were looking for an opportunity to kill him. Now the Jewish festival of Booths was near. . . . But after his brothers had gone to the festival, then he also went, not publicly but as it were in secret. . . . Now some of the people of Jerusalem were saying, "Is not this the man whom they are trying to kill? And here he is, speaking openly, but they say nothing to him! Can it be that the authorities really know that this is the Messiah? Yet we know where this man is from; but when the Messiah comes, no one will know where he is from." Then Jesus cried out as he was teaching in the temple, "You know me, and you know where I am from. I have not come on my own. But the one who sent me is true, and you do not know him. I know him, because I am from him, and he sent me." Then they tried to arrest him, but no one laid hands on him, because his hour had not yet come.

- "Not publicly but as it were in secret"; Jesus never made himself the center. He was ever pointing to his Father and, toward the end of his life, speaking of the Spirit that was to come.

- "Yet we know where this man is from." In what ways do my biases—about a person's race, language, religion, or country of origin—prevent my listening to what the person actually says? I pray for openness to receive God's words when they reach me—and however they reach me.

Saturday 28th March
John 7:40–53

When they heard these words, some in the crowd said, "This is really the prophet." Others said, "This is the Messiah." But some asked, "Surely the Messiah does not come from Galilee, does he? Has not the scripture said that the Messiah is descended from David and comes from Bethlehem, the village where David lived?" So there was a division in the crowd because of him. Some of them wanted to arrest him, but no one laid hands on him. Then the temple police went back to the chief priests and Pharisees, who asked them, "Why did you not arrest him?" The police answered, "Never has anyone spoken like this!" Then the Pharisees replied, "Surely you have not been deceived too, have you? Has any one of the authorities or of the Pharisees believed in him? But this crowd, which does not know the law—they are accursed." Nicodemus, who had gone to Jesus before, and who was one of them, asked, "Our law does not judge people without first giving them a hearing to find out what they are doing, does it?" They replied, "Surely you are not also from Galilee, are you? Search and you will see that no prophet is to arise from Galilee." Then each of them went home.

- According to Meister Eckhart, the great medieval theologian and mystic, the Son of God is being born unceasingly: "If God stopped saying his Word, but for an instant even, heaven and earth would disappear." That Word of God is spoken in my soul. When I stop to listen to it, I am in touch with the source of all creation.

- Prayer can allow us to be surprised by Jesus Christ—or to be questioned by him. We can end our prayer with the question, "Who is this man, and what have I learned about him today?" He gives no easy answers but walks with us while we ask the questions.

March 29—April 4

Something to think and pray about each day this week:

Real peace is not just a matter of structures and mechanisms. It rests, above all, on the adoption of a style of human coexistence marked by mutual acceptance and a capacity to forgive from the heart. We all need to be forgiven by others, so we must all be ready to forgive. Asking and granting forgiveness is something profoundly worthy of every one of us; sometimes it is the only way out of situations marked by age-old and violent hatred.

Forgiveness, in its truest and highest form, is a free act of love; but precisely because it is an act of love, it has its own intrinsic demands: the first of which is respect for the truth.

God alone is absolute truth, but He made the human heart open to the desire for truth, which He then fully revealed in His Incarnate Son. Hence, we are all called to live the truth. Forgiveness, far from precluding the search for truth, actually requires it. Evil that has been done must be acknowledged and, as far as possible, corrected.

—Saint John Paul II, *Go in Peace*

The Presence of God
God is with me, but even more astounding, God is within me.
Let me dwell for a moment on God's life-giving presence
in my body, in my mind, in my heart,
as I sit here, right now.

Freedom
Lord, may I never take the gift of freedom for granted. You gave me the great blessing of freedom of spirit. Fill my spirit with your peace and joy.

Consciousness
I remind myself that I am in the presence of God, who is my strength in times of weakness and my comforter in times of sorrow.

The Word
I take my time to read the word of God slowly, a few times, allowing myself to dwell on anything that strikes me. (Please turn to the Scripture on the following pages. Inspiration points are there, should you need them. When you are ready, return here to continue.)

Conversation

Jesus, you always welcomed little children when you walked on this earth. Teach me to have a childlike trust in you. Teach me to live in the knowledge that you will never abandon me.

Conclusion

Glory be to the Father, and to the Son, and to the Holy Spirit,
As it was in the beginning, is now and ever shall be,
World without end. Amen.

Sunday 29th March
Fifth Sunday of Lent
John 11:3–7, 17, 20–27, 33b–45

So the sisters sent a message to Jesus, "Lord, he whom you love is ill." But when Jesus heard it, he said, "This illness does not lead to death; rather it is for God's glory, so that the Son of God may be glorified through it." Accordingly, though Jesus loved Martha and her sister and Lazarus, after having heard that Lazarus was ill, he stayed two days longer in the place where he was. Then after this he said to the disciples, "Let us go to Judea again." . . . When Jesus arrived, he found that Lazarus had already been in the tomb four days. . . . When Martha heard that Jesus was coming, she went and met him, while Mary stayed at home. Martha said to Jesus, "Lord, if you had been here, my brother would not have died. But even now I know that God will give you whatever you ask of him." Jesus said to her, "Your brother will rise again." Martha said to him, "I know that he will rise again in the resurrection on the last day." Jesus said to her, "I am the resurrection and the life. Those who believe in me, even though they die, will live, and everyone who lives and believes in me will never die. Do you believe this?" She said to him, "Yes, Lord, I believe that you are the Messiah, the Son of God, the one coming into the world." . . . When Jesus saw

[Mary] weeping, and the Jews who came with her also weeping, he was greatly disturbed in spirit and deeply moved. He said, "Where have you laid him?" They said to him, "Lord, come and see." Jesus began to weep. So the Jews said, "See how he loved him!" But some of them said, "Could not he who opened the eyes of the blind man have kept this man from dying?" Then Jesus, again greatly disturbed, came to the tomb. It was a cave, and a stone was lying against it. Jesus said, "Take away the stone." Martha, the sister of the dead man, said to him, "Lord, already there is a stench because he has been dead for four days." Jesus said to her, "Did I not tell you that if you believed, you would see the glory of God?" So they took away the stone. And Jesus looked upward and said, "Father, I thank you for having heard me. I knew that you always hear me, but I have said this for the sake of the crowd standing here, so that they may believe that you sent me." When he had said this, he cried with a loud voice, "Lazarus, come out!" The dead man came out, his hands and feet bound with strips of cloth, and his face wrapped in a cloth. Jesus said to them, "Unbind him, and let him go." Many of the Jews therefore, who had come with Mary and had seen what Jesus did, believed in him.

- I hear you asking me the same question, Lord: "Do you believe that I am the resurrection and the life?" In the long run, nothing is more important than my answer to this. I cannot grasp your words in my imagination, Lord, but I believe. Help my unbelief.

- "Unbind him, and let him go." Even a man resurrected from the dead needed the help of community. Show me, Lord, how I can participate in others' unbinding and freedom.

Monday 30th March
John 8:1–11

Jesus went to the Mount of Olives. Early in the morning Jesus came again to the temple. All the people came to him and he sat down and began to teach them. The scribes and the Pharisees brought a woman who had been caught in adultery; and making her stand before all of them, they said to him, "Teacher, this woman was caught in the very act of committing adultery. Now in the law Moses commanded us to stone such women. Now what do you say?" They said this to test him, so that they might have some charge to bring against him. Jesus bent down and wrote with his finger on the ground. When they kept on questioning him, he straightened up and said to them, "Let anyone among you who is without sin be the first to throw a stone at her." And once again he bent down and wrote on the ground. When they heard it, they went away, one by one, beginning with the elders; and Jesus was left alone with the woman standing before him. Jesus straightened up and said to her, "Woman, where are they? Has no one condemned you?" She said, "No one, sir." And Jesus said, "Neither do I condemn you. Go your way, and from now on do not sin again."

- We have all sinned. We have all experienced overwhelming shame. Even if the sin is not discovered, our self-accusatory voice can become so loud in our head that it drowns out the gentle voice of Jesus, telling us to begin again.

- If we cannot believe ourselves forgiven, how will we ever be able to move out of what the philosopher Ivan Illich describes as "our self-imposed cages"? Lord, you who opened the ears of the deaf and the eyes of the blind, let me hear your words of forgiveness; let me see and believe in the possibility of a better life.

Tuesday 31st March
John 8:21–30

Again he said to them, "I am going away, and you will search for me, but you will die in your sin. Where I am going, you cannot come." Then the Jews said, "Is he going to kill himself? Is that what he means by saying, 'Where I am going, you cannot come'?"

He said to them, "You are from below, I am from above; you are of this world, I am not of this world. I told you that you would die in your sins, for you will die in your sins unless you believe that I am he." They said to him, "Who are you?" Jesus said to them, "Why do I speak to you at all? I have much to say about you and much to condemn; but the one who sent me is true, and I declare to the world what I have heard from him." They did not understand that he was speaking to them about the Father. So Jesus said, "When you have lifted up the Son of Man, then you will realize that I am he, and that I do nothing on my own, but I speak these things as the Father instructed me. And the one who sent me is with me; he has not left me alone, for I always do what is pleasing to him." As he was saying these things, many believed in him.

- "I am going away, and you will search for me, but you will die in your sin." The time to search for Jesus is now. If I want to see how closely my daily life is aligned with my life priorities, I need only ask myself one question: "How do I spend my time?" What do I do most, and what are the things I postpone? What do I think about most? Aspire to most?

- If our hearts and our lives are tied to this world, can we really be seeking Christ?

Wednesday 1st April

John 8:31–42

Then Jesus said to the Jews who had believed in him, "If you continue in my word, you are truly my disciples; and you will know the truth, and the truth will make you free." They answered him, "We are descendants of Abraham and have never been slaves to anyone. What do you mean by saying, 'You will be made free'?" Jesus answered them, "Very truly, I tell you, everyone who commits sin is a slave to sin. The slave does not have a permanent place in the household; the son has a place there forever. So if the Son makes you free, you will be free indeed. I know that you are descendants of Abraham; yet you look for an opportunity to kill me, because there is no place in you for my word. I declare what I have seen in the Father's presence; as for you, you should do what you have heard from the Father." They answered him, "Abraham is our father." Jesus said to them, "If you were Abraham's children, you would be doing what Abraham did, but now you are trying to kill me, a man who has told you the truth that I heard from God. This is not what Abraham did. You are indeed doing what your father does." They said to him, "We are not illegitimate children; we have one father, God himself." Jesus said to them, "If God were your Father, you would love me, for I came from

God and now I am here. I did not come on my own, but he sent me."

- "Abiding" ("continue in") means that we draw life from the word of God. This life is Christ himself; he is the love of the Father. Being a disciple, a listener, is living and abiding in truth, knowing that the Jesus of our prayer comes from God and is with God.

- Our love indicates our spiritual pedigree. Jesus, help me follow you and thus accept truth and demonstrate it through love.

Thursday 2nd April

John 8:51–59

Jesus said, "Very truly, I tell you, whoever keeps my word will never see death." The Jews said to him, "Now we know that you have a demon. Abraham died, and so did the prophets; yet you say, 'Whoever keeps my word will never taste death.' Are you greater than our father Abraham, who died? The prophets also died. Who do you claim to be?" Jesus answered, "If I glorify myself, my glory is nothing. It is my Father who glorifies me, he of whom you say, 'He is our God,' though you do not know him. But I know him; if I were to say that I do not know him, I would be a liar like you. But I do know him and I keep his word. Your ancestor Abraham rejoiced that he would see my day; he saw it and was glad." Then the Jews said to him, "You are not yet fifty years old, and have you seen Abraham?" Jesus said to them, "Very truly, I tell you, before Abraham was, I am." So they picked up stones to throw at him, but Jesus hid himself and went out of the temple.

- The wilderness inside us is a place of testing, where the power of false gods is broken. It is a place of encounter with ourselves, with our inner demons, and with God. To enter it, we must be silent and alone, leaving behind our elaborately constructed avoidance techniques, safety nets, and empty spiritual practices. Only through making ourselves vulnerable to our own pain and fear can we make ourselves open to the experience of loving and of being loved.

- Note yet another "I am" statement: *Before Abraham was, I am.* Jesus claims both preexistence and oneness with God. How does such information influence the way I think about life and death and what it means to be a spiritual being?

Friday 3rd April
John 10:31–42

The Jews took up stones again to stone him. Jesus replied, "I have shown you many good works from the Father. For which of these are you going to stone me?" The Jews answered, "It is not for a good work that we are going to stone you, but for blasphemy, because you, though only a human being, are making yourself God." Jesus answered, "Is it not written in your law, 'I said, you are gods'? If those to whom the word of God came were called 'gods'—and the scripture cannot be annulled—can you say that the one whom the Father has sanctified and sent into the world is blaspheming because I said, 'I am God's Son'? If I am not doing the works of my Father, then do not believe me. But if I do them, even though you do not believe me, believe the works, so that you may know and understand that the Father is in me and I am in the Father." Then they tried to arrest him again, but he escaped from their hands. He went away again across the Jordan to the place where John had been baptizing earlier, and he remained there. Many came to him, and they were saying, "John performed no sign, but everything that John said about this man was true." And many believed in him there.

- Jesus often impresses upon us the need to act upon his word. One can argue with words, but deeds cannot be contradicted. They speak for themselves. The Word is planted deep in me, and I pray in the words of the apostle James, "Let me be a doer of the word, and not a forgetful hearer." The world watches the deeds of Christians—and often is not impressed.

- The people in today's reading condemn Jesus because of their particular image of God. What is my image of God? Have I ever condemned someone because I nursed a warped image of God?

Saturday 4th April

John 11:45–56

Many of the Jews therefore, who had come with Mary and had seen what Jesus did, believed in him. But some of them went to the Pharisees and told them what he had done. So the chief priests and the Pharisees called a meeting of the council, and said, "What are we to do? This man is performing many signs. If we let him go on like this, everyone will believe in him, and the Romans will come and destroy both our holy place and our nation." But one of them, Caiaphas, who was high priest that year, said to them, "You know nothing at all! You do not understand that it is better for you to have one man die for the people than to have the whole nation destroyed." He did not say this on his own, but being high priest that year he prophesied that Jesus was about to die for the nation, and not for the nation only, but to gather into one the dispersed children of God. So from that day on they planned to put him to death. Jesus therefore no longer walked about openly among the Jews, but went from there to a town called Ephraim in the region near the wilderness; and he remained there with the disciples. Now the Passover of the Jews was near, and many went up from the country to Jerusalem before the Passover to purify themselves. They were looking for Jesus and were asking one another as they stood in the temple, "What do you think? Surely he will not come to the festival, will he?"

- Caiaphas was a Sadducee. He was also ruthless, political, and determined to buttress the status quo and the privileges of his wealthy class. He used the argument of the powerful in every age: we must eliminate the awkward troublemaker in the name of the common good—in this case, "the common good" meaning the comfort of the Sadducees. But he spoke wiser than he knew. One man, Jesus, was to die for the people, and for me.

- Caiaphas is afraid that the popularity of Jesus will draw down the wrath of Rome and destroy both the temple—the holy place—and the nation. In his blindness he cannot see that the Jewish people are themselves the temple. Do I appreciate that I, too, am a temple of the living God? Lord, take away my blindness so that I can see myself as you see me.

April 5—April 11

Something to think and pray about each day this week:

Ingenuity blossoms when the personal freedom to pursue opportunities is linked to a profound trust and optimism that the world presents plenty of them. Imagination, creativity, adaptability, and rapid response become the keys for finding and unlocking those opportunities.

—Chris Lowney, *Heroic Leadership*

The Presence of God

Dear Lord, as I come to you today, fill my heart, my whole being, with the wonder of your presence. Help me remain receptive to you as I put aside the cares of this world. Fill my mind with your peace.

Freedom

Lord, grant me the grace to be free from the excesses of this life. Let me not get caught up with the desire for wealth. Keep my heart and mind free to love and serve you.

Consciousness

I exist in a web of relationships: links to nature, people, God.

I trace out these links, giving thanks for the life that flows through them.

Some links are twisted or broken; I may feel regret, anger, disappointment.

I pray for the gift of acceptance and forgiveness.

The Word

God speaks to each of us individually. I listen attentively to hear what he is saying to me. Read the text a few times, then listen. (Please turn to the Scripture on the following pages. Inspiration points are there, should you need them. When you are ready, return here to continue.)

Conversation
Jesus, you speak to me through the words of the Gospels. May I respond to your call today. Teach me to recognize your hand at work in my daily living.

Conclusion
I thank God for these moments we have spent together and for any insights I have been given concerning the text.

Sunday 5th April
Palm Sunday of the Passion of the Lord
Matthew 27:45–54

From noon on, darkness came over the whole land until three in the afternoon. And about three o'clock Jesus cried with a loud voice, "Eli, Eli, lema sabachthani?" that is, "My God, my God, why have you forsaken me?" When some of the bystanders heard it, they said, "This man is calling for Elijah." At once one of them ran and got a sponge, filled it with sour wine, put it on a stick, and gave it to him to drink. But the others said, "Wait, let us see whether Elijah will come to save him." Then Jesus cried again with a loud voice and breathed his last. At that moment the curtain of the temple was torn in two, from top to bottom. The earth shook, and the rocks were split. The tombs also were opened, and many bodies of the saints who had fallen asleep were raised. After his resurrection they came out of the tombs and entered the holy city and appeared to many. Now when the centurion and those with him, who were keeping watch over Jesus, saw the earthquake and what took place, they were terrified and said, "Truly this man was God's Son!"

- People expected the Messiah to be a hero figure— one whom Elijah would miraculously deliver at the last minute. Indeed, if Jesus had been delivered from the cross, no doubt the religious leaders who put him there would have proclaimed him the Messiah. But Jesus is not a savior who delivers himself from the reality humanity must face. His life demonstrated the holy nature—made in God's image—of the human race. And Jesus of Nazareth would make redemptive even the act of dying.

- Watch the scene here: the death of the good man. Allow yourself to be touched by it; let Jesus die for you and for all. Then look at the one guarding the cross— the one who says that this Man was God's Son. In prayer express your belief and faith in this truth.

Monday 6th April

John 12:1–11

Six days before the Passover Jesus came to Bethany, the home of Lazarus, whom he had raised from the dead. There they gave a dinner for him. Martha served, and Lazarus was one of those at the table with him. Mary took a pound of costly perfume made of pure nard, anointed Jesus' feet, and wiped them with her hair. The house was filled with the fragrance of the perfume. But Judas Iscariot, one of his disciples (the one who was about to betray him), said, "Why was this perfume not sold for three hundred denarii and the money given to the poor?" (He said this not because he cared about the poor, but because he was a thief;

he kept the common purse and used to steal what was put into it.) Jesus said, "Leave her alone. She bought it so that she might keep it for the day of my burial. You always have the poor with you, but you do not always have me." When the great crowd of the Jews learned that he was there, they came not only because of Jesus but also to see Lazarus, whom he had raised from the dead. So the chief priests planned to put Lazarus to death as well, since it was on account of him that many of the Jews were deserting and were believing in Jesus.

- We join the dinner party and are struck by the surpassing generosity of Mary's gesture, and then by the bitter begrudging with which Judas interprets the gift. We might allow moments of prayer this week to reach the zones within us that need tolerance, healing, and forgiveness.

- The generosity of Mary appeared wasteful and misplaced. Mary knew that Jesus was worthy of her honor and service, even when it cost. She was not held back by the judgments of others. Jesus, may I give to you freely and not care about others' opinions and reactions.

Tuesday 7th April
John 13:21–33, 36–38

After saying this Jesus was troubled in spirit, and declared, "Very truly, I tell you, one of you will betray me." The disciples looked at one another, uncertain of whom he was speaking. One of his disciples—the one whom Jesus loved—was reclining next to him; Simon Peter therefore motioned to him to ask Jesus of whom he was speaking. So while reclining next to Jesus, he asked him, "Lord, who is it?" Jesus answered, "It is the one to whom I give this piece of bread when I have dipped it in the dish." So when he had dipped the piece of bread, he gave it to Judas son of Simon Iscariot. After he received the piece of bread, Satan entered into him. Jesus said to him, "Do quickly what you are going to do." Now no one at the table knew why he said this to him. Some thought that, because Judas had the common purse, Jesus was telling him, "Buy what we need for the festival"; or, that he should give something to the poor. So, after receiving the piece of bread, he immediately went out. And it was night. When he had gone out, Jesus said, "Now the Son of Man has been glorified, and God has been glorified in him. If God has been glorified in him, God will also glorify him in himself and will glorify him at once. Little children, I am with you only a little longer. You will look for me; and as I said to the Jews so now I say to you, 'Where I am going, you cannot come.'" . . . Simon Peter said to him, "Lord, where are you going?" Jesus answered, "Where I am going, you cannot follow me now; but you will follow afterward." Peter said to him, "Lord, why can I not follow you now? I will lay down my life for you." Jesus answered, "Will you lay down your life for me? Very truly, I tell you, before the cock crows, you will have denied me three times."

- We rightly hesitate to answer affirmatively the question: "Will you lay down your life for me?" But there is no ambivalence in Jesus. He has already decided to lay down his life for us, in purest love.

- Imagine yourself at the table during the Last Supper. Are you picking up the tensions among the other participants? Do you notice how Jesus is troubled in spirit? Let the drama of the scene draw you into it. What are your predominant feelings? Speak freely to Jesus about the whole situation and your reactions to it.

Wednesday 8th April
Matthew 26:14–25

Then one of the twelve, who was called Judas Iscariot, went to the chief priests and said, "What will you give me if I betray him to you?" They paid him thirty pieces of silver. And from that moment he began to look for an opportunity to betray him. On the first day of Unleavened Bread the disciples came to Jesus, saying, "Where do you want us to make the preparations for you to eat the Passover?" He said,

"Go into the city to a certain man, and say to him, 'The Teacher says, My time is near; I will keep the Passover at your house with my disciples.'" So the disciples did as Jesus had directed them, and they prepared the Passover meal. When it was evening, he took his place with the twelve; and while they were eating, he said, "Truly I tell you, one of you will betray me." And they became greatly distressed and began to say to him one after another, "Surely not I, Lord?" He answered, "The one who has dipped his hand into the bowl with me will betray me. The Son of Man goes as it is written of him, but woe to that one by whom the Son of Man is betrayed! It would have been better for that one not to have been born." Judas, who betrayed him, said, "Surely not I, Rabbi?" He replied, "You have said so."

- In some places this day is known as Spy Wednesday. Judas is the spy or sly, sneaky person who secretly approaches the chief priests with the intention of betraying Jesus to them. Jesus uses only words to persuade Judas not to carry out his pact with the chief priests. He takes no other measures to prevent his arrest. What is your reaction to this?

- Like us, Judas didn't see that it is we, not God, who must change. The real sin of Judas was not his betrayal but his rejection of the light. Judas refused to believe in the possibility of forgiveness.

Let us not imitate him. No matter what wrong we have done, we can turn to Jesus for forgiveness and healing.

Thursday 9th April
Holy Thursday
John 13:1–15

Now before the festival of the Passover, Jesus knew that his hour had come to depart from this world and go to the Father. Having loved his own who were in the world, he loved them to the end. The devil had already put it into the heart of Judas son of Simon Iscariot to betray him. And during supper Jesus, knowing that the Father had given all things into his hands, and that he had come from God and was going to God, got up from the table, took off his outer robe, and tied a towel around himself. Then he poured water into a basin and began to wash the disciples' feet and to wipe them with the towel that was tied around him. He came to Simon Peter, who said to him, "Lord, are you going to wash my feet?" Jesus answered, "You do not know now what I am doing, but later you will understand." Peter said to him, "You will never wash my feet." Jesus answered, "Unless I wash you, you have no share with me." Simon Peter said to him, "Lord, not my feet only but also my hands and my head!" Jesus said to him,

"One who has bathed does not need to wash, except for the feet, but is entirely clean. And you are clean, though not all of you." For he knew who was to betray him; for this reason he said, "Not all of you are clean." After he had washed their feet, had put on his robe, and had returned to the table, he said to them, "Do you know what I have done to you? You call me Teacher and Lord—and you are right, for that is what I am. So if I, your Lord and Teacher, have washed your feet, you also ought to wash one another's feet. For I have set you an example, that you also should do as I have done to you."

- Jesus kneels at my feet, as he did at Peter's, and he addresses the same words to me: "Unless I wash you, you have no share with me." But have I the courage and the generosity to accept his forgiveness and unconditional love?

- Lord, let my response to your love always be an unfaltering "Yes!"

Friday 10th April
Good Friday
John 18:1—19:42

After Jesus had spoken these words, he went out with his disciples across the Kidron valley to a place where there was a garden, which he and his disciples entered. Now Judas, who betrayed him, also knew the place, because Jesus often met there with his disciples. So Judas brought a detachment of soldiers together with police from the chief priests and the Pharisees, and they came there with lanterns and torches and weapons. Then Jesus, knowing all that was to happen to him, came forward and asked them, "Whom are you looking for?" They answered, "Jesus of Nazareth." Jesus replied, "I am he." Judas, who betrayed him, was standing with them. When Jesus said to them, "I am he," they stepped back and fell to the ground. Again he asked them, "Whom are you looking for?" And they said, "Jesus of Nazareth." Jesus answered, "I told you that I am he. So if you are looking for me, let these men go." This was to fulfill the word that he had spoken, "I did not lose a single one of those whom you gave me." Then Simon Peter, who had a sword, drew it, struck the high priest's slave, and cut off his right ear. The slave's name was Malchus. Jesus said to Peter, "Put your sword back into its sheath. Am I not to drink the cup that the Father has given me?"

So the soldiers, their officer, and the Jewish police arrested Jesus and bound him. First they took him to Annas, who was the father-in-law of Caiaphas, the high priest that year. Caiaphas was the one who had advised the Jews that it was better to have one person die for the people.

Simon Peter and another disciple followed Jesus. Since that disciple was known to the high priest, he went with Jesus into the courtyard of the high priest, but Peter was standing outside at the gate. So the other disciple, who was known to the high priest, went out, spoke to the woman who guarded the gate, and brought Peter in. The woman said to Peter, "You are not also one of this man's disciples, are you?" He said, "I am not." Now the slaves and the police had made a charcoal fire because it was cold, and they were standing around it and warming themselves. Peter also was standing with them and warming himself.

Then the high priest questioned Jesus about his disciples and about his teaching. Jesus answered, "I have spoken openly to the world; I have always taught in synagogues and in the temple, where all the Jews come together. I have said nothing in secret. Why do you ask me? Ask those who heard what I said to them; they know what I said." When he had said this, one of the police standing nearby struck Jesus on the face, saying, "Is that how you answer the high priest?" Jesus answered, "If I have spoken wrongly, testify to the wrong. But if I have spoken rightly, why do you strike me?" Then Annas sent him bound to Caiaphas the high priest.

Now Simon Peter was standing and warming himself. They asked him, "You are not also one of his disciples, are you?" He denied it and said, "I am not."

One of the slaves of the high priest, a relative of the man whose ear Peter had cut off, asked, "Did I not see you in the garden with him?" Again Peter denied it, and at that moment the cock crowed.

Then they took Jesus from Caiaphas to Pilate's headquarters. It was early in the morning. They themselves did not enter the headquarters, so as to avoid ritual defilement and to be able to eat the Passover. So Pilate went out to them and said, "What accusation do you bring against this man?" They answered, "If this man were not a criminal, we would not have handed him over to you." Pilate said to them, "Take him yourselves and judge him according to your law." The Jews replied, "We are not permitted to put anyone to death." (This was to fulfill what Jesus had said when he indicated the kind of death he was to die.)

Then Pilate entered the headquarters again, summoned Jesus, and asked him, "Are you the King of the Jews?" Jesus answered, "Do you ask this on your own, or did others tell you about me?" Pilate replied, "I am not a Jew, am I? Your own nation and the chief priests have handed you over to me. What have you done?" Jesus answered, "My kingdom is not from this world. If my kingdom were from this world, my followers would be fighting to keep me from being handed over to the Jews. But as it is, my kingdom is not from here." Pilate asked him, "So you are a king?" Jesus answered, "You say that I am a king. For this I was born, and for this I came into the world, to testify to the truth. Everyone who belongs to the truth listens to my voice." Pilate asked him, "What is truth?"

After he had said this, he went out to the Jews again and told them, "I find no case against him." But you have a custom that I release someone for you at the Passover. Do you want me to release for you the King of the Jews?" They shouted in reply, "Not this man, but Barabbas!" Now Barabbas was a bandit.

Then Pilate took Jesus and had him flogged. And the soldiers wove a crown of thorns and put it on his head, and they dressed him in a purple robe. They kept coming up to him, saying, "Hail, King of the Jews!" and striking him on the face. Pilate went out again and said to them, "Look, I am bringing him out to you to let you know that I find no case against him." So Jesus came out, wearing the crown of thorns and the purple robe. Pilate said to them, "Here is the man!" When the chief priests and the police saw him, they shouted, "Crucify him! Crucify him!" Pilate said to them, "Take him yourselves and crucify him; I find no case against him." The Jews answered him, "We have a law, and according to that law he ought to die because he has claimed to be the Son of God."

Now when Pilate heard this, he was more afraid than ever. He entered his headquarters again and asked Jesus, "Where are you from?" But Jesus gave him no answer. Pilate therefore said to him, "Do you refuse to speak to me? Do you not know that I have power to release you, and power to crucify you?" Jesus answered him, "You would have no power over me unless it had been given you from above; therefore the one who handed me over to you is guilty of a greater sin." From then on Pilate tried to release him, but the Jews cried out, "If you release this man, you are no friend of the emperor. Everyone who claims to be a king sets himself against the emperor."

When Pilate heard these words, he brought Jesus outside and sat on the judge's bench at a place called The Stone Pavement, or in Hebrew Gabbatha. Now it was the day of Preparation for the Passover; and it was about noon. He said to the Jews, "Here is your King!" They cried out, "Away with him! Away with him! Crucify him!" Pilate asked them, "Shall I crucify your King?" The chief priests answered, "We have no king but the emperor." Then he handed him over to them to be crucified.

So they took Jesus; and carrying the cross by himself, he went out to what is called The Place of the Skull, which in Hebrew is called Golgotha. There they crucified him, and with him two others, one on either side, with Jesus between them. Pilate also had an inscription written and put on the cross. It read, "Jesus of Nazareth, the King of the Jews." Many of the Jews read this inscription, because the place where Jesus was crucified was near the city; and it was written in Hebrew, in Latin, and in Greek. Then the chief priests of the Jews said to Pilate, "Do not write, 'The King of the Jews,' but, 'This man said, I am King of the Jews.'" Pilate answered, "What I have written I have written." When the soldiers had crucified Jesus, they took his clothes and divided them into four parts, one for each soldier. They also took his tunic; now the tunic was seamless, woven in one piece from the top. So they said to one another, "Let us not tear it, but cast lots for it to see who will get it." This was to fulfill what the scripture says, "They divided my clothes among themselves, / and for my clothing they cast lots." And that is what the soldiers did.

Meanwhile, standing near the cross of Jesus were his mother, and his mother's sister, Mary the wife of Clopas, and Mary Magdalene. When Jesus saw his mother and the disciple whom he loved standing beside her, he said to his mother, "Woman, here is your son." Then he said to the disciple, "Here is your mother." And from that hour the disciple took her into his own home.

After this, when Jesus knew that all was now finished, he said (in order to fulfill the scripture), "I am thirsty." A jar full of sour wine was standing there. So they put a sponge full of the wine on a branch of hyssop and held it to his mouth. When Jesus had received the wine, he said, "It is finished." Then he bowed his head and gave up his spirit.

Since it was the day of Preparation, the Jews did not want the bodies left on the cross during the sabbath, especially because that sabbath was a day of great solemnity. So they asked Pilate to have the legs of the crucified men broken and the bodies removed. Then the soldiers came and broke the legs of the first and of the other who had been crucified with him. But when they came to Jesus and saw that he was already dead, they did not break his legs. Instead, one of the soldiers pierced his side with a spear, and at once blood and water came out. (He who saw this has testified so that you also may believe. His testimony is true, and he knows that he tells the truth.) These things occurred so that the scripture might be fulfilled, "None of his bones shall be broken." And again another passage of scripture says, "They will look on the one whom they have pierced."

After these things, Joseph of Arimathea, who was a disciple of Jesus, though a secret one because of his fear of the Jews, asked Pilate to let him take away the body of Jesus. Pilate gave him permission; so he came and removed his body. Nicodemus, who had at first come to Jesus by night, also came, bringing a mixture of myrrh and aloes, weighing about a hundred pounds. They took the body of Jesus and wrapped it with the spices in linen cloths, according to the burial custom of the Jews. Now there was a garden in the place where he was crucified, and in the garden there was a new tomb in which no one had ever been laid. And so, because it was the Jewish day of Preparation, and the tomb was nearby, they laid Jesus there.

- Good Friday puts the cross before me and challenges me not to look away. If I have followed Jesus' footsteps to Calvary, I do not have to fear because I, like him, am confident in God's enduring presence. Wherever there is suffering or pain, I seek the face of Jesus. I ask him for the strength I need to be a sign of hope wherever there is despair, to be a presence of love wherever it is most needed.

- All of us will one day give up our spirit. In prayer we can offer our death to God; we can do so with Mary: "Holy Mary, mother of God, pray for us, sinners; now and at the hour of our death."

Saturday 11th April
Holy Saturday
Matthew 28:1–10

After the sabbath, as the first day of the week was dawning, Mary Magdalene and the other Mary went to see the tomb. And suddenly there was a great earthquake; for an angel of the Lord, descending from heaven, came and rolled back the stone and sat on it. His appearance was like lightning, and his clothing white as snow. For fear of him the guards shook and became like dead men. But the angel said to the women, "Do not be afraid; I know that you are looking for Jesus who was crucified. He is not here; for he has been raised, as he said. Come, see the place where he lay. Then go quickly and tell his disciples, 'He has been raised from the dead, and indeed he is going ahead of you to Galilee; there you will see him.' This is my message for you." So they left the tomb quickly with fear and great joy, and ran to tell his disciples. Suddenly Jesus met them and said, "Greetings!" And they came to him, took hold of his feet, and worshiped him. Then Jesus said to them, "Do not be afraid; go and tell my brothers to go to Galilee; there they will see me."

- The angel and Jesus say to the women, "Do not be afraid." Change, revelation, and enlightenment tempt us to be anxious because we have encountered something so beyond our understanding. Jesus, help me remember "Do not be afraid" when I sense a transformation beginning in my life.

- Another point in common between the angel and Jesus is that they instructed the women to go tell the other disciples. Our life with Jesus is personal but not private; the Good News is meant to be shared. Am I willing to share this treasure in my life?

April 12

Something to think and pray about each day this week:

Decision making is a struggle, yet the Ignatian approach accepts the struggle wholeheartedly. In fact, the approach to decision making that Ignatius suggests depends on this struggle. It claims that the signs of God's direction for our lives are found precisely in the shifting movements of our divided hearts as spiritual forces struggle for mastery. Ignatian discernment teaches us to become aware of those movements, to reflect on them, and to interpret them. The battle is the problem, but it is also the solution.

—J. Michael Sparough, SJ, Jim Manney, and Tim Hipskind, SJ, *What's Your Decision?*

The Presence of God
Dear Jesus, today I call on you, but not to ask for anything. I'd like only to dwell in your presence. May my heart respond to your love.

Freedom
God my creator, you gave me life and the gift of freedom. Through your love I exist in this world. May I never take the gift of life for granted. May I always respect others' right to life.

Consciousness
I ask how I am today. Am I particularly tired, stressed, or anxious? If any of these characteristics apply, can I try to let go of the concerns that disturb me?

The Word
The word of God comes down to us through the Scriptures. May the Holy Spirit enlighten my mind and my heart to respond to the Gospel teachings. (Please turn to the Scripture on the following page. Inspiration points are there, should you need them. When you are ready, return here to continue.)

Conversation
I begin to talk with Jesus about the Scripture I have just read. What part of it strikes a chord in me?

Perhaps the words of a friend—or some story I have heard recently—will rise to the surface in my consciousness. If so, does the story throw light on what the Scripture passage may be saying to me?

Conclusion
Glory be to the Father, and to the Son, and to the Holy Spirit,
As it was in the beginning, is now and ever shall be,
World without end. Amen.

Sunday 12th April
Easter Sunday of the Resurrection of the Lord

John 20:1–9

Early on the first day of the week, while it was still dark, Mary Magdalene came to the tomb and saw that the stone had been removed from the tomb. So she ran and went to Simon Peter and the other disciple, the one whom Jesus loved, and said to them, "They have taken the Lord out of the tomb, and we do not know where they have laid him." Then Peter and the other disciple set out and went toward the tomb. The two were running together, but the other disciple outran Peter and reached the tomb first. He bent down to look in and saw the linen wrappings lying there, but he did not go in. Then Simon Peter came, following him, and went into the tomb. He saw the linen wrappings lying there, and the cloth that had been on Jesus' head, not lying with the linen wrappings but rolled up in a place by itself. Then the other disciple, who reached the tomb first, also went in, and he saw and believed; for as yet they did not understand the scripture, that he must rise from the dead.

- "We proclaim the resurrection of Christ," says Pope Francis, "when his light illuminates the dark moments of our existence, and we are able to share it with others; when we know when to smile with those who smile, and weep with those who weep; when we accompany those who are sad and at risk of losing hope; when we recount our experience of Faith to those who are searching for meaning and happiness . . . and there—with our attitude, with our witness, with our life—we say 'Jesus is risen,' with our soul."

- Neither Peter nor John come to believe in the Resurrection without enduring confusion and uncertainty. But out of the confusion comes clarity. The empty tomb can only mean that Jesus is truly alive—raised and transformed by the Father. If Jesus is truly risen, then so are we. As we were one with him in his suffering, so are we now one with him in his risen joy. Alleluia!

Suscipe

Take, Lord, and receive all my liberty,
my memory, my understanding,
and my entire will,

all I have and call my own.
You have given all to me.

To you, Lord, I return it.
Everything is yours; do with it what you will.
Give me only your love and your grace;
that is enough for me.

—St. Ignatius of Loyola

Prayer to Know God's Will

May it please the supreme and divine Goodness
To give us all abundant grace
Ever to know his most holy will
And perfectly to fulfill it.

—St. Ignatius of Loyola